Just for Today

A Journal for Conscious Living

By Wendy Craig-Purcell

unity®
Books

Unity Village, Missouri

Just for Today
First Edition 2019

Unity Books are available at special discounts for bulk purchases
for study groups, book clubs, sales promotions, book signings,
or fundraising. To place an order, call the Unity Customer Care
Department at 816-251-3571 or email *ccwholesale@unityonline.org*.

Cover design: Laura Carl
Interior design: Laura Carl

ISBN: 978-0-87159-400-6
Library of Congress Control Number: 2019946300
Canada BN: 13252 0933 RT

Preface

Several years ago, I began a new spiritual practice. Each morning as I emerge from meditation, I write a few sentences about my intention for the day—not so much what I intend to *do* but how I want to *be*. Each day's contemplation becomes a practice that I share with the world via email and social media.

For this journal, I selected 101 of my most powerful practices. I've paired them with beautiful designs and open space. This format allows you to reflect on and explore this practice in your own life. I hope what began as my personal challenge now serves you on your own spiritual journey.

What I know is this: Anytime any one of us chooses to practice living from a more spiritually aware and centered place, we not only begin to transform our lives, we also help heal our world.

Blessings,
Wendy Craig-Purcell

You can find me on Twitter *@reverendwendy.*

Dedication

To all those committed to their spiritual journey …
one step, one day, one mindful practice at a time.

With very special thanks to ...

My daughter, Jennifer, for retrieving nearly four years' worth of *Just for Today* messages so I could select the ones to include in this journal. Without your help, this journal would still be only an idea.

To my son, Johnathon, who models the very best of what it means to be a conscious, awakened male.

To my husband, John, for knowing that pretty much every single morning—no matter what—I would be in my meditation chair waiting to receive and then write *Just for Today*. I feel your support and encouragement every day.

To Kim Kennedy, Jenna Rowe, and Ken Fendrick for your personal support of me and your contagious enthusiasm for this project.

To Joan Woods-Petties for the warmest hugs on the planet.

To Yvette Stanley for being the very first to suggest these *Just for Today* messages be turned into a journal.

Just for Today

I practice living the entire day well. I set—and keep resetting if necessary—the tone for today. Conditions are not always mine to choose, but attitude *is* mine to choose!

Just for Today

I practice bringing the light from within me to shine on all who are on my path. I joyfully do my part in creating a world that works for everyone with every thought I think and action I take.

Just for Today

I practice viewing obstacles and challenges through the eyes of faith. I ask myself: *What good might be happening behind the scenes or beneath the surface that I simply can't see right now?*

Just for Today

I look at my world through spiritually alert and awake eyes. Today I look deeper and longer. I look beyond appearances. I look beyond my stories. I look beyond my judgments.

Just for Today

I practice living from deep, spiritual wisdom. I stop allowing things I have no control over physically to control me emotionally. I surrender and let go. I allow peace to flow through me now.

Just for Today

My guiding word is appreciation. I practice being more aware of what I appreciate in others *and* in myself. Today I will not only tell at least three people what I appreciate about them, I will also reflect on what I appreciate about myself.

Just for Today

I will find the goodness in every moment, every situation, and every person—even the ones I don't like. Especially the ones I don't like.

15

Just for Today

I will practice being more peaceful and patient. No matter how frustrating the situation, how slow the person, or how disappointing the news, I will see it for what it is spiritually. It is a call to practice patience, and I am determined to get a passing grade.

Just for Today

I practice patience with myself. As I move forward toward the changes I want to make in my life, I gently remind myself that I cannot change overnight something that took my entire life to build.

Just for Today

I stop being an emotional *sherpa*. I stop schlepping around emotional baggage from the past. My journey will be much lighter, easier, and more joyful when I stop carrying the pain of the past with me. I bring the learning forward but leave the pain behind.

Just for Today

I practice being more open. My mind is open to new ways of thinking. My heart is open to new ways of being. My hands are open to new ways of serving and making a difference. Today I am open.

Just for Today

I show up as a spiritual researcher in my own life by asking myself a better question. I let faith, not fear, carry me into the answer. Rather than asking, *What could go wrong?* I will ask myself, *What could go right?*

Just for Today

I practice deep, spiritual self-care. I stop fighting with myself. I stop being my own worst enemy. I ease up. I am gently and lovingly firm with myself, confident that this is a more successful path to a life of true meaning and purpose.

27

Just for Today

I choose to come from love. Whether it's a decision
I have to make, a conversation I need to have, or
an action I have to take, I choose to come from love.

Just for Today

I practice leaving every situation better than I found it.
I leave every place I go more peaceful than when I
arrived and leave every conversation at a higher
vibration than when it began.

Just for Today

I practice dancing with change. I stop waiting for things to quiet down or turn around. Instead I start moving with meaning and flowing with faith. I can trust the rhythm of life and the undercurrent of love.

Just for Today

I deepen my practice of gratitude. What in this person have I not noticed before that I can appreciate? What in the course of my day do I take for granted? Let me appreciate it now. What comes easily to me now that was once difficult? Let me appreciate how I've grown.

Just for Today

I recognize and celebrate that I am a unique expression of the Infinite. As I remember who I was before others told me who I should be, I give myself the freedom to be authentically and fully me.

Just for Today

I practice spiritual patience. At times the divine guidance I seek may be slow in coming. At those times I let go and make room for Spirit to work through and around me, trusting that other things may need to happen first and then answers will come at the perfect time.

Just for Today

I pay attention to what is showing up in my life. I don't resist or turn away. I am fully present. I look more deeply. I remember everything comes up either to be healed or to bless me. Even that which needs healing eventually blesses me.

Just for Today

I practice perspective by looking at things differently. I lift my vision above the appearance of limitation to the infinite field of possibility. I stop freeze-framing the places where I seem to be stuck and instead take the long view of what I'm working toward.

Just for Today

I practice taking better care of myself. What good habit can I strengthen today? What bad habit can I weaken? Every thought I think and every choice I make is an opportunity to practice better self-care.

Just for Today

I think on purpose. I put myself on a healthy mental diet and choose my thoughts with intention. Good or bad, happy or sad, loving or fearful, my thoughts always deliver results. Today I choose thoughts that will create the tomorrow I want to live in.

Just for Today

I make friends with silence and emptiness. In stillness, I embrace the unknown. I stop rushing to try to figure everything out. I give my life a chance to surprise me.

Just for Today

I do my inner work first. If I'm tempted to blame, judge, or criticize anyone, I will stop first, look within, and ask: *What is this really about for me? What in me is this triggering? Why am I holding the thoughts I'm holding?* I do my own work first.

Just for Today

I make sure I do not major in minors, make mountains out of molehills, or call a pity party when things don't go my way. I challenge myself to ask: *Was it really a bad day or week? Or was it just a bad incident that I rehashed all day?*

Just for Today

I practice looking at my life as a piece of art. At times I've been more conscious of my creation than at other times. Every thought I think, decision I make, and action I take adds a brushstroke. Today I approach the canvas of my life with an artist's eye.

Just for Today

I evaluate where and how I am investing my life energy. Thought by thought, decision by decision, and action by action, I build my life by what I value, what I allow, and what I focus on. Am I satisfied with my return? Does my life portfolio need rebalancing?

Just for Today

I practice staying true to the deeper calling of my soul. There is work I am meant to do, people I am meant to serve, and gifts I am meant to give. As I listen to that deeper call, my path becomes clear and my way becomes easy.

Just for Today

I trust in the underlying flow of divine order operating in the universe. Even if it is not obvious to my eyes, I know there is a wisdom and intelligence at work within and all around me. When I've done all that is mine to do, I let go and trust.

Just for Today

I practice being whatever is missing. If a situation becomes tense, I practice being peaceful. If a conversation turns nasty, I practice being a unifying presence. If a problem seems unsolvable, I practice being resourceful. My *beingness* makes a difference.

Just for Today

I open up to new ways of looking at things, especially challenging situations, new opportunities, or big changes. How might this look to a curious child? To a wise elder? To a fully awakened being? A new perspective can change how I feel and how I act.

Just for Today

I practice being my true, authentic self. I connect with others not where I am pretending to be strong, but where I am open and vulnerable. I give up trying to be perfect. I allow myself to be who I truly am and then grow from there.

Just for Today

I practice paying attention to what gets my attention, especially the things that annoy or upset me. Beneath the resistance and upset there is a story I am telling myself. My mantra today is: The more I look, the more I unhook.

Just for Today

I approach the difficulties in my life with a spirit of curiosity, a heart of compassion, and a mind of wisdom. What can I learn about myself? What unexpected good might be hiding? What greater Truth is waiting to be revealed?

Just for Today

I practice gratitude for every step that brought me to this place in my life. I give thanks for doors that opened and even those that shut. I give thanks for people who came and even those who left. Every experience showed me something about myself and helped me grow.

Just for Today

I surrender and trust. Surrender isn't about giving up; it's about being open. Trust isn't blind faith; it's knowing there is a force for good in the universe and choosing to align with it.

Just for Today

I practice living life as if everything is rigged in my favor.
I am allowed to be prosperous. I am allowed to live an
abundant life. I am allowed to live my life with ease and
grace and enjoy every minute of it.

Just for Today

Gratitude is my guiding word and practice today. The many and varied activities of my day are like beads on a necklace. Gratitude is the string that holds them together. If only for a brief moment, I pause between each activity, breathe, and silently say *thank you.*

Just for Today

I practice being a student. My mind is open, my heart is willing, and I am fully present to the deeper truths my life is trying to teach me. I recognize that everyone and everything is my teacher and plays a role in my spiritual growth.

Just for Today

I practice simplicity. I stop overthinking, overdoing, and overconsuming. I know what to say *yes* to, what to say *no* to, and what to say *not now* to. Simplicity leaves me less stressed and much happier.

Just for Today

I practice moving at the pace of loving-kindness. If I notice I am moving too fast or simply trying to fit too much in my day—making me unable to respond to others in a patient, kind, and respectful way—I slow down and consciously change my pace.

Just for Today

I exercise my power to choose. I may or may not like where I am in my life now. I may or may not understand how I got here. But today I will remember the very real, life-changing power I have. I can—and will—choose where I go from here.

Just for Today

I pay attention to my inner guidance. As I listen to the whisper of my soul, my learning is gentle. No longer do I need to be awakened by a cosmic two-by-four. No longer am I spiritually hard of hearing. I will trust my intuition and follow my passion.

Just for Today

I stop holding myself hostage to my past. I am not the mistakes I've made. I am not the limiting stories I've accepted about myself. I am something more. Much more. I start trusting that "something more" and let it reveal my true and unique magnificence.

Just for Today

I practice mindfulness. Like water, when my mind is agitated it is difficult to see beyond the surface. When my mind is quiet and calm, the answer becomes clear. I remind myself that quiet and calm are only a few breaths away.

Just for Today

I stop letting other people or situations determine how I feel. No one and nothing can *make* me feel anything. No one and nothing can drive me crazy unless I accept the passenger seat!

Just for Today

I choose to keep believing in myself and take another step forward. Just because I'm not yet *where* I want to be or *how* I want to be can't keep me from getting there—unless I give up. As long as I keep believing in myself, I can keep moving forward.

Just for Today

I practice being an encourager. In every conversation or communication, I find at least one encouraging thing to say. My positive words, attitude, and energy change the vibration around me. Today I am a cheerleader of all that is good and all that is possible.

Just for Today

I use my words as skillfully as a surgeon uses a scalpel. I speak words that bring harmony where I see discord, hope where I see discouragement, clarity where I see chaos, and understanding where I see intolerance.

Just for Today

I cultivate inner peace. Things may or may not go the way I plan. People may or may not show up the way I think they should. No matter the outer condition, I can cultivate inner peace with this simple mantra: The peace I seek is in the breath I breathe.

Just for Today

I bring a spiritual awareness to everything I do—even the mundane, routine tasks of my life. *Especially* the mundane, routine tasks of my life. Whatever is mine to do today, I do lovingly and mindfully.

Just for Today

I "practice the pause." If I find myself stressed, I will practice the pause. If I'm worried, I will practice the pause. If I'm afraid, I will practice the pause. If I'm angry, I will practice the pause. In the pause, I will breathe and pray.

Just for Today

I give up and make way. I give up limiting beliefs and make way for brand-new possibilities. I give up fear and make way for courage. I give up complaining and make way for appreciating. Today I give up the negative to make way for the positive.

Just for Today

I practice tenderness. I look with the eyes of tenderness and see the light behind appearances. I listen with the ears of tenderness and hear Truth beneath the fear. I move through the day with the energy of tenderness, and my day unfolds with ease and grace.

Just for Today

I practice listening. Really listening. Listening deeply. When family or friends or coworkers need to talk, I am present. With my actions—and perhaps with my words —I affirm: *I am listening. Take all the time you need.*

Just for Today

I practice letting go. Whether it's simply exhaling deeply, moving away physically, or moving on emotionally, I listen for the whisper that says, "Let go." I carry the lesson forward, leaving the pain and struggle behind.

Just for Today

I practice seeing every encounter, every conversation, and every activity as an opportunity for my spiritual growth. As I go through my day, my silent mantra will be: May this experience open my heart and awaken my soul.

Just for Today

I give myself a precious gift by practicing forgiveness.
As I forgive, my mind becomes clear, my heart opens,
my soul is set free, and a new path opens before me.

Just for Today

I practice making a fresh start and stepping forward in faith. No matter what my past has been, my future is spotless. Today is a new day. This *now* moment is the beginning of anything I really want.

Just for Today

I practice moving confidently and steadily toward my goals. The overall direction—not speed—of my steps is important. Going slowly is not a problem; standing still when I *could* take a step is the only problem.

Just for Today

I practice walking in faith and courage toward my dreams. I will not be fooled by appearances or stopped by obstacles. I will challenge my soul to go beyond what my eyes can see.

Just for Today

I practice staying centered, calm, and grounded no matter how much I have to do or what is going on around me. I stop focusing on how stressed I am and remember instead how blessed I am.

Just for Today

I practice being gentle and kind. My thoughts are nonjudgmental, my words are uplifting, and my actions are supportive. I will not let the challenges of these times cause me to treat others with anything less than kindness and respect.

Just for Today

I raise my vibration through a more active, conscious practice of gratitude. Every stoplight, long line, or time waiting on hold is a golden opportunity to breathe in love and breathe out gratitude.

Just for Today

I practice leaning into joys as well as challenges with a soft heart, calm mind, and open spirit. I remember that at every twist and turn, every up and down in my life, I have the opportunity to stretch and grow, evolve and unfold.

Just for Today

I check myself for excess baggage. I don't like paying for extra baggage when I fly, so why would I carry it as I fly through life? Am I still nursing a grudge? Harboring a resentment? Rehearsing a drama? It's time to leave it behind.

Just for Today

I listen as an act of true loving-kindness and respect. I do not stay quiet, simply waiting for my chance to reply. I stay quiet to hold space and listen deeply to others so I may be influenced by what they have to say.

Just for Today

I bring a joyful energy to everyone I meet and everything I do. I remind myself my mood isn't dependent upon anything external. Though it may not always be easy, the truth is that I can choose to practice any feeling I desire. Today I practice joyfulness.

Just for Today

I practice spiritual "volume control." I turn the volume down on the negative chatter in my mind; I turn the volume up on the steady but quiet voice of possibility in my heart. What I have envisioned in faith I will not let the voice of doubt destroy.

Just for Today

I take myself a little less seriously. I stop making things bigger than they really are. As I take a deep breath, smile, and relax into the good that is trying to emerge, I find I can trust the process of life a whole lot more.

Just for Today

I move forward with enthusiasm. Every day is a new beginning. I will not get stuck in what might have been but stay joyfully open and present to what can be. I make a fresh start by bringing a clear mind and an open heart to the day.

Just for Today

I will practice centering myself and rebalancing my day. I will spend some time hanging out in the space between my thoughts and in the stillness between my breaths.

Just for Today

I practice being more open and receptive. I am willing to examine the ideas and opinions I defend, realizing that whatever I cling to makes me unavailable to hear anything new.

Just for Today

I practice being guided by my faith rather than held hostage by my fears. Whatever is mine to do, whatever is mine to face, whatever is mine to heal, whatever is mine to overcome, let my mantra simply be: Breathe and believe.

Just for Today

I go for personal greatness. As I approach each person, each task, and each situation today, I challenge myself to bring the very best of me forward mentally, emotionally, and spiritually.

Just for Today

I practice turning within and looking forward. Rather than trying to build a brighter tomorrow by resurrecting the old, I look within for the fresh and new that is trying to emerge. I only need to give it time and space and a little faith.

Just for Today

I return to center. Just as there is a space of quiet and calm in the eye of the storm, so, too, there is a space within me that is quiet and calm no matter what is going on around me. At my center I know who I am, I know what I want, I know what to do.

Just for Today

I practice being an openhearted, safe space where others can be their authentic selves. I listen with kindness and speak with warmth. I may be the only place today where another can truly feel seen and heard.

Just for Today

I center myself in God's flow of unconditional love. As I breathe in love and breathe out gratitude, my every breath becomes a prayer that brings me into the realization I am safe and all is well.

Just for Today

I practice moving forward, onward, and upward, one choice and one step at a time. I will not let the distance between where I am today and where I want to be discourage me from taking the step before me now.

Just for Today

I practice being in this moment. This instant is holy and sacred. This instant is the birthplace of all the good I long to bring forth. From the peace and clarity I find in this moment, I move forward with wisdom and faith and courage.

Just for Today

I let go of all that weighs me down and I celebrate my own special spirit. I may have to let go again and again and again, but each time I do, my unique light shines brighter and I discover newfound strength and joy.

Just for Today

I live at a saner, more peaceful pace. I slow down.
I quiet the chatter of my mind and lower the volume
of the outside world. I tune in to my inner being.
Today I mentally unplug and spiritually reboot my soul.

Just for Today

I hold a vision for my life that is not limited by my past nor hampered by where I am today. I choose carefully the thoughts I think and the messages I listen to. I will not let fear decide my future. I let curiosity open the way and faith guide my steps.

Just for Today

I watch where I direct my mental and emotional energy, especially when trying to move through painful experiences, meet challenging situations, or deal with difficult people. Let me remember that when I focus on the hurt, I suffer, but when I focus on the lesson, I grow.

Just for Today

I practice being more creative. I set my mind free to approach my life—even routine responsibilities—with more creativity. I stretch my thinking and open my imagination. I stop being afraid of being wrong or making a mistake. I let my inner child out to play.

Just for Today

I practice cultivating deep inner peace by quieting my mind and opening my heart. When my mind is noisy or judging, it is difficult to see; when it is quiet, everything suddenly becomes clear. With a few cleansing, centering breaths, my heart will show me the way.

Just for Today

I look for the good in everyone and everything. It's often easy to see. Sometimes it's buried beneath fear or pain or disguised as a lesson to be learned or a skill to be mastered. No matter how hard it is to see, I can and do trust that good is there.

Just for Today

I step back a bit to notice the overall texture and feel of my life. With every thought I think and decision I make, I am building my life. What I value, what I allow, and what I focus on becomes the life I am living. Is it time to make any changes?

Just for Today

I practice being calm. If something frustrating has happened or someone has said something upsetting, I quickly return to center with a conscious breath. Interruptions and inconveniences become opportunities for me to pause, breathe, and become mindful.

Just for Today

I hold my problems in a new light. Rather than seeing problems as merely something to be solved, I see them as the training ground for my spiritual growth and awakening. They become the very places where I discover who and what I really am.

Just for Today

I purposely slow down and become more aware. I try moving through my day as if it were a gift to explore rather than a race to be run or a list to complete. Could I drive a bit slower? Walk more mindfully? Breathe more deeply? Eat more consciously? Yes!

Just for Today

I let go and relax into my day. Knowing there is potential good in every situation, I loosen my grip a bit. Remembering there is a rhythm and flow of order beneath any seeming chaos, I adjust my pace and move with a sense of ease and grace.

Just for Today

I move through my day with a grateful heart. What do I see around me that I am grateful for? What sounds do I hear that I appreciate? Who crosses my path and blesses my day in some small way? An active practice of gratitude resets my day.

Just for Today

I make choices that reflect my dreams—not my doubts—choices that leave the pain behind but carry the learning forward. A better tomorrow begins and ends with the choices I make now. Today I choose more consciously.

Just for Today

I look within and let go. Are negative thoughts, limiting beliefs, or painful stories holding me hostage? Are unhealthy habits or destructive behaviors keeping me from a better life? That may have been true up until now, but today I make a fresh start.

Printed in U.S.A.

B0141